Glorifying Grace Prayer Journal Men's Edition
By Imani M-Glover & Cedric B. Glover
Published by Imani M-Glover
Under Sophisticated Press LLC

PRINTED IN THE UNITED STATES OF AMERICA

Book Design by Sophisticated Press LLC
ISBN 978-0-578-51587-8

Scriptures marked NIV are taken from the NEW INTERNATIONAL VERSION (NIV): Scripture taken from THE HOLY BIBLE, NEW INTERNATIONAL VERSION ®. Copyright© 1973, 1978, 1984, 2011 by Biblica, Inc.™. Used by permission of Zondervan

SOPHISTICATED
PRESS

Acknowledgements

To my soulmate Imani Glover Who I adore and admire and love with all my heart and soul. Thank you to my Mom Hattie M. Glover thank you for your love, wisdom, and knowledge.

To my boys : Solomon Glover Thank you for having a kind heart and beautiful spirit. Thank you Kwame' Glover for your wisdom and discernment. Baby Z, thank you for bringing sunshine and love into our home.

My sister Monica Glover, thank you for all your faith and support.

Thank you Brother Eric for staying strong in Christ and supporting the Glovers with this project.

Cedric B. Glover

Acknowledgements

Special thanks to the following people that supported this project. The Holy Spirit, my Husband Cedric G., my late Mother Lucy, my son Solomon G., my son Kwame' G., my grandmother Rosa Lee , Work Bible Studies w/ Valarie Mathews, my Aunt Ernestine, Acts Full Gospel Church, Declare Victory prayer call (Dionne Jackson), San Diego Bible Study w/ Pastor Edith, Marriage Matters prayer call, Sophisticated Press LLC, Wives Who War sisters, Dawn King, LaSonda McDuffie and Cassandra Weatherby. I would like to thank Barbara Marshall. To all of my family and close friends, thank you for your support whether you have taken my phone calls, listen to me vent, supported me, encouraged me, prayed with me or for me, and most importantly loved up on me.

Imani M-Glover

Foreword

It is my extreme honor and pleasure to be asked to write about the men's edition of Glorifying Grace Prayer Journal. It is with grace and a desire to see men of God bring their visions, reflections, and prayers into focus that prompted Imani Glover and her Husband Cedric Glover to write this book.

It is my sincere hope and prayer that this book will help men to organize their thoughts, petitions, and refine their ears to hear God's word for them while they endeavor as in Jeremiah 30:2 to "write in a book all the words I have spoken unto you."

May you be like the prophet Habakkuk, and write your vision, make it plain, using this journal as a tool to help you run with it!

God Bless,

Eric Smith

2019 Calendar

January

S	M	T	W	T	F	S
		1	2	3	4	5
6	7	8	9	10	11	12
13	14	15	16	17	18	19
20	21	22	23	24	25	26
27	28	29	30	31		

February

S	M	T	W	T	F	S
					1	2
3	4	5	6	7	8	9
10	11	12	13	14	15	16
17	18	19	20	21	22	23
24	25	26	27	28		

March

S	M	T	W	T	F	S
					1	2
3	4	5	6	7	8	9
10	11	12	13	14	15	16
17	18	19	20	21	22	23
24	25	26	27	28	29	30
31						

April

S	M	T	W	T	F	S
	1	2	3	4	5	6
7	8	9	10	11	12	13
14	15	16	17	18	19	20
21	22	23	24	25	26	27
28	29	30				

May

S	M	T	W	T	F	S
			1	2	3	4
5	6	7	8	9	10	11
12	13	14	15	16	17	18
19	20	21	22	23	24	25
26	27	28	29	30	31	

June

S	M	T	W	T	F	S
						1
2	3	4	5	6	7	8
9	10	11	12	13	14	15
16	17	18	19	20	21	22
23	24	25	26	27	28	29
30						

July

S	M	T	W	T	F	S
	1	2	3	4	5	6
7	8	9	10	11	12	13
14	15	16	17	18	19	20
21	22	23	24	25	26	27
28	29	30	31			

August

S	M	T	W	T	F	S
				1	2	3
4	5	6	7	8	9	10
11	12	13	14	15	16	17
18	19	20	21	22	23	24
25	26	27	28	29	30	31

September

S	M	T	W	T	F	S
1	2	3	4	5	6	7
8	9	10	11	12	13	14
15	16	17	18	19	20	21
22	23	24	25	26	27	28
29	30					

October

S	M	T	W	T	F	S
		1	2	3	4	5
6	7	8	9	10	11	12
13	14	15	16	17	18	19
20	21	22	23	24	25	26
27	28	29	30	31		

November

S	M	T	W	T	F	S
					1	2
3	4	5	6	7	8	9
10	11	12	13	14	15	16
17	18	19	20	21	22	23
24	25	26	27	28	29	30

December

S	M	T	W	T	F	S
1	2	3	4	5	6	7
8	9	10	11	12	13	14
15	16	17	18	19	20	21
22	23	24	25	26	27	28
29	30	31				

 *Important Dates*

1 January — New Year's Day
21 January — MLK Birthday
14 February — Valentine Day
18 February — President's Day
21 April — Easter Day
12 May — Mother's Day
27 May — Memorial Day
16 June — Father's Day
4 July — Independence Day
2 September — Labor Day
11 November — Veteran's Day
28 November — Thanksgiving Day
24 December — Christmas Eve
25 December — Christmas Day

Let Us Pray

Prayer Journal

TITLE: _____ DATE: _____ / _____ / _____

RELEVANT SCRIPTURES:

1. _____ 2. _____ 3. _____
4. _____ 5. _____ 6. _____

CONTENT OF PRAYER REQUEST

_____
_____
_____
_____

THE LORDS ANSWER WAS: DATE: _____ / _____ / _____
YES
NO
NOT YET

HOW THE LORD ANSWERED MY PRAYER

_____
_____
_____
_____

DETAIL OF DELIVERY / LESSON LEARNED

_____
_____
_____
_____

SIGNATURE OF ACCOUNTABILITY _____

PSALM 23:1 THE LORD IS MY SHEPHERD, I LACK NOTHING.

Prayer Journal

TITLE: _____ DATE: _____ / _____ / _____

RELEVANT SCRIPTURES:

1. _____ 2. _____ 3. _____
4. _____ 5. _____ 6. _____

CONTENT OF PRAYER REQUEST

_____
_____
_____
_____

THE LORDS ANSWER WAS: DATE: _____ / _____ / _____
YES
NO
NOT YET

HOW THE LORD ANSWERED MY PRAYER

_____
_____
_____
_____

DETAIL OF DELIVERY / LESSON LEARNED

_____
_____
_____
_____

SIGNATURE OF ACCOUNTABILITY _____

Prayer Journal

TITLE: _____   DATE: _____ / _____ / _____

RELEVANT SCRIPTURES:

1. _____ 2. _____ 3. _____
4. _____ 5. _____ 6. _____

CONTENT OF PRAYER REQUEST

_____
_____
_____
_____

THE LORDS ANSWER WAS: DATE: _____ / _____ / _____
YES
NO
NOT YET

HOW THE LORD ANSWERED MY PRAYER

_____
_____
_____
_____

DETAIL OF DELIVERY / LESSON LEARNED

_____
_____
_____
_____

SIGNATURE OF ACCOUNTABILITY _____

PSALM 23:2 HE MAKES ME LIE DOWN IN GREEN PASTURES,
HE LEADS ME BESIDE QUIET WATERS,

Prayer Journal

TITLE: _____   DATE: _____ / _____ / _____

RELEVANT SCRIPTURES:

1. _____ 2. _____ 3. _____
4. _____ 5. _____ 6. _____

CONTENT OF PRAYER REQUEST

_____
_____
_____
_____

THE LORDS ANSWER WAS: DATE: _____ / _____ / _____
YES
NO
NOT YET

HOW THE LORD ANSWERED MY PRAYER

_____
_____
_____
_____

DETAIL OF DELIVERY / LESSON LEARNED

_____
_____
_____
_____

SIGNATURE OF ACCOUNTABILITY _____

Prayer Journal

TITLE: _____ DATE: _____ / _____ / _____

RELEVANT SCRIPTURES:

1. _____ 2. _____ 3. _____
4. _____ 5. _____ 6. _____

CONTENT OF PRAYER REQUEST

_____
_____
_____
_____

THE LORDS ANSWER WAS: DATE: _____ / _____ / _____
YES
NO
NOT YET

HOW THE LORD ANSWERED MY PRAYER

_____
_____
_____
_____

DETAIL OF DELIVERY / LESSON LEARNED

_____
_____
_____
_____

SIGNATURE OF ACCOUNTABILITY _____

PSALM 23:3 HE REFRESHES MY SOUL. HE GUIDES ME ALONG THE RIGHT PATHS FOR HIS NAME'S SAKE.

Prayer Journal

TITLE: _____ DATE: _____ / _____ / _____

RELEVANT SCRIPTURES:

1. _____ 2. _____ 3. _____
4. _____ 5. _____ 6. _____

CONTENT OF PRAYER REQUEST

_____
_____
_____
_____

THE LORDS ANSWER WAS: DATE: _____ / _____ / _____
YES
NO
NOT YET

HOW THE LORD ANSWERED MY PRAYER

_____
_____
_____
_____

DETAIL OF DELIVERY / LESSON LEARNED

_____
_____
_____
_____

SIGNATURE OF ACCOUNTABILITY _____

Prayer Journal

TITLE: _____   DATE: _____ / _____ / _____

RELEVANT SCRIPTURES:

1. _____ 2. _____ 3. _____
4. _____ 5. _____ 6. _____

CONTENT OF PRAYER REQUEST

_____
_____
_____
_____

THE LORDS ANSWER WAS: DATE: _____ / _____ / _____
YES
NO
NOT YET

HOW THE LORD ANSWERED MY PRAYER

_____
_____
_____
_____

DETAIL OF DELIVERY / LESSON LEARNED

_____
_____
_____
_____

SIGNATURE OF ACCOUNTABILITY _____

PSALM 23:4 EVEN THOUGH I WALK THROUGH THE DARKEST VALLEY, [A]
I WILL FEAR NO EVIL, FOR YOU ARE WITH ME; YOUR ROD AND YOUR STAFF, THEY COMFORT ME.

Prayer Journal

TITLE: _____ DATE: _____ / _____ / _____

RELEVANT SCRIPTURES:

1. _____ 2. _____ 3. _____
4. _____ 5. _____ 6. _____

CONTENT OF PRAYER REQUEST

_____
_____
_____
_____

THE LORDS ANSWER WAS: DATE: _____ / _____ / _____
YES
NO
NOT YET

HOW THE LORD ANSWERED MY PRAYER

_____
_____
_____
_____

DETAIL OF DELIVERY / LESSON LEARNED

_____
_____
_____
_____

SIGNATURE OF ACCOUNTABILITY _____

Prayer Journal

TITLE: _____   DATE: _____ / _____ / _____

RELEVANT SCRIPTURES:

1. _____ 2. _____ 3. _____
4. _____ 5. _____ 6. _____

CONTENT OF PRAYER REQUEST

_____
_____
_____
_____

THE LORDS ANSWER WAS: DATE: _____ / _____ / _____
YES
NO
NOT YET

HOW THE LORD ANSWERED MY PRAYER

_____
_____
_____
_____

DETAIL OF DELIVERY / LESSON LEARNED

_____
_____
_____
_____

SIGNATURE OF ACCOUNTABILITY _____

PSALM 23:5 YOU PREPARE A TABLE BEFORE ME IN THE PRESENCE OF MY ENEMIES.
YOU ANOINT MY HEAD WITH OIL; MY CUP OVERFLOWS.

Prayer Journal

TITLE: _____   DATE: _____ / _____ / _____

RELEVANT SCRIPTURES:

1. _____ 2. _____ 3. _____
4. _____ 5. _____ 6. _____

CONTENT OF PRAYER REQUEST

_____
_____
_____
_____

THE LORDS ANSWER WAS: DATE: _____ / _____ / _____
YES
NO
NOT YET

HOW THE LORD ANSWERED MY PRAYER

_____
_____
_____
_____

DETAIL OF DELIVERY / LESSON LEARNED

_____
_____
_____
_____

SIGNATURE OF ACCOUNTABILITY _____

Prayer Journal

TITLE: _____ DATE: _____ / _____ / _____

RELEVANT SCRIPTURES:

1. _____ 2. _____ 3. _____
4. _____ 5. _____ 6. _____

CONTENT OF PRAYER REQUEST

_____
_____
_____
_____

THE LORDS ANSWER WAS: DATE: _____ / _____ / _____
YES
NO
NOT YET

HOW THE LORD ANSWERED MY PRAYER

_____
_____
_____
_____

DETAIL OF DELIVERY / LESSON LEARNED

_____
_____
_____
_____

SIGNATURE OF ACCOUNTABILITY _____

PSALM 23:6 SURELY YOUR GOODNESS AND LOVE WILL FOLLOW ME ALL THE DAYS OF MY LIFE, AND I WILL DWELL IN THE HOUSE OF THE LORD FOREVER.

Prayer Journal

TITLE: _____ DATE: _____ / _____ / _____

RELEVANT SCRIPTURES:

1. _____ 2. _____ 3. _____
4. _____ 5. _____ 6. _____

CONTENT OF PRAYER REQUEST

_____

_____

_____

_____

THE LORDS ANSWER WAS: DATE: _____ / _____ / _____
YES
NO
NOT YET

HOW THE LORD ANSWERED MY PRAYER

_____

_____

_____

_____

DETAIL OF DELIVERY / LESSON LEARNED

_____

_____

_____

_____

SIGNATURE OF ACCOUNTABILITY _____

Prayer Journal

TITLE: _____   DATE: _____ / _____ / _____

RELEVANT SCRIPTURES:

1. _____ 2. _____ 3. _____
4. _____ 5. _____ 6. _____

CONTENT OF PRAYER REQUEST

_____
_____
_____
_____

THE LORDS ANSWER WAS: DATE: _____ / _____ / _____
YES
NO
NOT YET

HOW THE LORD ANSWERED MY PRAYER

_____
_____
_____
_____

DETAIL OF DELIVERY / LESSON LEARNED

_____
_____
_____
_____

SIGNATURE OF ACCOUNTABILITY _____

PHILIPIANS 4:1 THEREFORE, MY BROTHERS AND SISTERS, YOU WHOM
I LOVE AND LONG FOR, MY JOY AND CROWN, STAND FIRM IN THE LORD IN THIS WAY, DEAR FRIENDS!

Prayer Journal

TITLE: _____ DATE: _____ / _____ / _____

RELEVANT SCRIPTURES:

1. _____ 2. _____ 3. _____
4. _____ 5. _____ 6. _____

CONTENT OF PRAYER REQUEST

_____
_____
_____
_____

THE LORDS ANSWER WAS: DATE: _____ / _____ / _____
YES
NO
NOT YET

HOW THE LORD ANSWERED MY PRAYER

_____
_____
_____
_____

DETAIL OF DELIVERY / LESSON LEARNED

_____
_____
_____
_____

SIGNATURE OF ACCOUNTABILITY _____

Prayer Journal

TITLE: _____   DATE: _____ / _____ / _____

RELEVANT SCRIPTURES:

1. _____ 2. _____ 3. _____
4. _____ 5. _____ 6. _____

CONTENT OF PRAYER REQUEST

_____
_____
_____
_____

THE LORDS ANSWER WAS: DATE: _____ / _____ / _____
YES
NO
NOT YET

HOW THE LORD ANSWERED MY PRAYER

_____
_____
_____
_____

DETAIL OF DELIVERY / LESSON LEARNED

_____
_____
_____
_____

SIGNATURE OF ACCOUNTABILITY _____

PHILIPIANS 4:21 GREET ALL GOD'S PEOPLE IN CHRIST JESUS. THE BROTHERS AND SISTERS WHO ARE WITH ME SEND GREETINGS.

Prayer Journal

TITLE: _____   DATE: _____ / _____ / _____

RELEVANT SCRIPTURES:

1. _____ 2. _____ 3. _____
4. _____ 5. _____ 6. _____

CONTENT OF PRAYER REQUEST

_____
_____
_____
_____

THE LORDS ANSWER WAS: DATE: _____ / _____ / _____
YES
NO
NOT YET

HOW THE LORD ANSWERED MY PRAYER

_____
_____
_____
_____

DETAIL OF DELIVERY / LESSON LEARNED

_____
_____
_____
_____

SIGNATURE OF ACCOUNTABILITY _____

Prayer Journal

TITLE: _____ DATE: _____ / _____ / _____

RELEVANT SCRIPTURES:

1. _____ 2. _____ 3. _____
4. _____ 5. _____ 6. _____

CONTENT OF PRAYER REQUEST

_____
_____
_____
_____

THE LORDS ANSWER WAS: DATE: _____ / _____ / _____
YES
NO
NOT YET

HOW THE LORD ANSWERED MY PRAYER

_____
_____
_____
_____

DETAIL OF DELIVERY / LESSON LEARNED

_____
_____
_____
_____

SIGNATURE OF ACCOUNTABILITY _____

PHILIPIANS 4:3 YES, AND I ASK YOU, MY TRUE COMPANION, HELP THESE WOMEN SINCE THEY HAVE CONTENDED AT MY SIDE IN THE CAUSE OF THE GOSPEL, ALONG WITH CLEMENT AND THE REST OF MY CO-WORKERS, WHOSE NAMES ARE IN THE BOOK OF LIFE.

Prayer Journal

TITLE: _____ DATE: _____ / _____ / _____

RELEVANT SCRIPTURES:

1. _____ 2. _____ 3. _____
4. _____ 5. _____ 6. _____

CONTENT OF PRAYER REQUEST

_____
_____
_____
_____

THE LORDS ANSWER WAS: DATE: _____ / _____ / _____
YES
NO
NOT YET

HOW THE LORD ANSWERED MY PRAYER

_____
_____
_____
_____

DETAIL OF DELIVERY / LESSON LEARNED

_____
_____
_____
_____

SIGNATURE OF ACCOUNTABILITY _____

Prayer Journal

TITLE: _____ DATE: _____ / _____ / _____

RELEVANT SCRIPTURES:
1. _____ 2. _____ 3. _____
4. _____ 5. _____ 6. _____

CONTENT OF PRAYER REQUEST

_____
_____
_____
_____

THE LORDS ANSWER WAS: DATE: _____ / _____ / _____
YES
NO
NOT YET

HOW THE LORD ANSWERED MY PRAYER

_____
_____
_____
_____

DETAIL OF DELIVERY / LESSON LEARNED

_____
_____
_____
_____

SIGNATURE OF ACCOUNTABILITY _____

PHILIPIANS 4:4 REJOICE IN THE LORD ALWAYS. I WILL SAY IT AGAIN: REJOICE!

Prayer Journal

TITLE: _____   DATE: _____ / _____ / _____

RELEVANT SCRIPTURES:

1. _____ 2. _____ 3. _____
4. _____ 5. _____ 6. _____

CONTENT OF PRAYER REQUEST

_____
_____
_____
_____

THE LORDS ANSWER WAS: DATE: _____ / _____ / _____
YES
NO
NOT YET

HOW THE LORD ANSWERED MY PRAYER

_____
_____
_____
_____

DETAIL OF DELIVERY / LESSON LEARNED

_____
_____
_____
_____

SIGNATURE OF ACCOUNTABILITY _____

Prayer Journal

TITLE: _____   DATE: _____ / _____ / _____

RELEVANT SCRIPTURES:

1. _____   2. _____   3. _____
4. _____   5. _____   6. _____

CONTENT OF PRAYER REQUEST

_____
_____
_____
_____

THE LORDS ANSWER WAS: DATE: _____ / _____ / _____
YES
NO
NOT YET

HOW THE LORD ANSWERED MY PRAYER

_____
_____
_____
_____

DETAIL OF DELIVERY / LESSON LEARNED

_____
_____
_____
_____

SIGNATURE OF ACCOUNTABILITY _____

PHILIPIANS 4:5 LET YOUR GENTLENESS BE EVIDENT TO ALL. THE LORD IS NEAR.

Prayer Journal

TITLE: _____ DATE: _____ / _____ / _____

RELEVANT SCRIPTURES:

1. _____ 2. _____ 3. _____
4. _____ 5. _____ 6. _____

CONTENT OF PRAYER REQUEST

_____
_____
_____
_____

THE LORDS ANSWER WAS: DATE: _____ / _____ / _____
YES
NO
NOT YET

HOW THE LORD ANSWERED MY PRAYER

_____
_____
_____
_____

DETAIL OF DELIVERY / LESSON LEARNED

_____
_____
_____
_____

SIGNATURE OF ACCOUNTABILITY _____

Prayer Journal

TITLE: _____ DATE: _____ / _____ / _____

RELEVANT SCRIPTURES:

1. _____ 2. _____ 3. _____
4. _____ 5. _____ 6. _____

CONTENT OF PRAYER REQUEST

_____
_____
_____
_____

THE LORDS ANSWER WAS: DATE: _____ / _____ / _____
YES
NO
NOT YET

HOW THE LORD ANSWERED MY PRAYER

_____
_____
_____
_____

DETAIL OF DELIVERY / LESSON LEARNED

_____
_____
_____
_____

SIGNATURE OF ACCOUNTABILITY _____

PHILIPIANS 4: 6 DO NOT BE ANXIOUS ABOUT ANYTHING, BUT IN EVERY SITUATION,
BY PRAYER AND PETITION, WITH THANKSGIVING, PRESENT YOUR REQUESTS TO GOD.

Prayer Journal

TITLE: _____ DATE: _____ / _____ / _____

RELEVANT SCRIPTURES:

1. _____ 2. _____ 3. _____
4. _____ 5. _____ 6. _____

CONTENT OF PRAYER REQUEST

_____
_____
_____
_____

THE LORDS ANSWER WAS: DATE: _____ / _____ / _____
YES
NO
NOT YET

HOW THE LORD ANSWERED MY PRAYER

_____
_____
_____
_____

DETAIL OF DELIVERY / LESSON LEARNED

_____
_____
_____
_____

SIGNATURE OF ACCOUNTABILITY _____

Prayer Journal

TITLE: _____ DATE: _____ / _____ / _____

RELEVANT SCRIPTURES:

1. _____ 2. _____ 3. _____
4. _____ 5. _____ 6. _____

CONTENT OF PRAYER REQUEST

_____
_____
_____
_____

THE LORDS ANSWER WAS: DATE: _____ / _____ / _____
YES
NO
NOT YET

HOW THE LORD ANSWERED MY PRAYER

_____
_____
_____
_____

DETAIL OF DELIVERY / LESSON LEARNED

_____
_____
_____
_____

SIGNATURE OF ACCOUNTABILITY _____

PHILIPIANS 4: 7 AND THE PEACE OF GOD, WHICH TRANSCENDS ALL
UNDERSTANDING, WILL GUARD YOUR HEARTS AND YOUR MINDS IN CHRIST JESUS.

Prayer Journal

TITLE: _____ DATE: _____ / _____ / _____

RELEVANT SCRIPTURES:

1. _____ 2. _____ 3. _____
4. _____ 5. _____ 6. _____

CONTENT OF PRAYER REQUEST

_____
_____
_____
_____

THE LORDS ANSWER WAS: DATE: _____ / _____ / _____
YES
NO
NOT YET

HOW THE LORD ANSWERED MY PRAYER

_____
_____
_____
_____

DETAIL OF DELIVERY / LESSON LEARNED

_____
_____
_____
_____

SIGNATURE OF ACCOUNTABILITY _____

Prayer Journal

TITLE: _____ DATE: _____ / _____ / _____

RELEVANT SCRIPTURES:

1. _____ 2. _____ 3. _____
4. _____ 5. _____ 6. _____

CONTENT OF PRAYER REQUEST

_____
_____
_____
_____

THE LORDS ANSWER WAS: DATE: _____ / _____ / _____
YES
NO
NOT YET

HOW THE LORD ANSWERED MY PRAYER

_____
_____
_____
_____

DETAIL OF DELIVERY / LESSON LEARNED

_____
_____
_____
_____

SIGNATURE OF ACCOUNTABILITY _____

PHILIPIANS 4: 8 FINALLY, BROTHERS AND SISTERS, WHATEVER IS TRUE, WHATEVER IS NOBLE, WHATEVER IS RIGHT, WHATEVER IS PURE, WHATEVER IS LOVELY, WHATEVER IS ADMIRABLE—IF ANYTHING IS EXCELLENT OR PRAISEWORTHY—THINK ABOUT SUCH THINGS.

Prayer Journal

TITLE: _____   DATE: _____ / _____ / _____

RELEVANT SCRIPTURES:

1. _____ 2. _____ 3. _____
4. _____ 5. _____ 6. _____

CONTENT OF PRAYER REQUEST

_____
_____
_____
_____

THE LORDS ANSWER WAS: DATE: _____ / _____ / _____
YES
NO
NOT YET

HOW THE LORD ANSWERED MY PRAYER

_____
_____
_____
_____

DETAIL OF DELIVERY / LESSON LEARNED

_____
_____
_____
_____

SIGNATURE OF ACCOUNTABILITY _____

Prayer Journal

TITLE: _____   DATE: _____ / _____ / _____

RELEVANT SCRIPTURES:

1. _____ 2. _____ 3. _____
4. _____ 5. _____ 6. _____

CONTENT OF PRAYER REQUEST

_____
_____
_____
_____

THE LORDS ANSWER WAS: DATE: _____ / _____ / _____
YES
NO
NOT YET

HOW THE LORD ANSWERED MY PRAYER

_____
_____
_____
_____

DETAIL OF DELIVERY / LESSON LEARNED

_____
_____
_____
_____

SIGNATURE OF ACCOUNTABILITY _____

PHILIPIANS 4: 9 WHATEVER YOU HAVE LEARNED OR RECEIVED OR HEARD FROM ME, OR SEEN IN ME—PUT IT INTO PRACTICE. AND THE GOD OF PEACE WILL BE WITH YOU.

Prayer Journal

TITLE: _____   DATE: _____ / _____ / _____

RELEVANT SCRIPTURES:

1. _____ 2. _____ 3. _____
4. _____ 5. _____ 6. _____

CONTENT OF PRAYER REQUEST

_____
_____
_____
_____

THE LORDS ANSWER WAS: DATE: _____ / _____ / _____
YES
NO
NOT YET

HOW THE LORD ANSWERED MY PRAYER

_____
_____
_____
_____

DETAIL OF DELIVERY / LESSON LEARNED

_____
_____
_____
_____

SIGNATURE OF ACCOUNTABILITY _____

Prayer Journal

TITLE: _____ DATE: _____ / _____ / _____

RELEVANT SCRIPTURES:

1. _____ 2. _____ 3. _____
4. _____ 5. _____ 6. _____

CONTENT OF PRAYER REQUEST

_____
_____
_____
_____

THE LORDS ANSWER WAS: DATE: _____ / _____ / _____
YES
NO
NOT YET

HOW THE LORD ANSWERED MY PRAYER

_____
_____
_____
_____

DETAIL OF DELIVERY / LESSON LEARNED

_____
_____
_____
_____

SIGNATURE OF ACCOUNTABILITY _____

PHILIPIANS 4:10 I REJOICED GREATLY IN THE LORD THAT AT LAST YOU RENEWED YOUR CONCERN FOR ME. INDEED, YOU WERE CONCERNED, BUT YOU HAD NO OPPORTUNITY TO SHOW IT.

Prayer Journal

TITLE: _____   DATE: _____ / _____ / _____

RELEVANT SCRIPTURES:

1. _____   2. _____   3. _____
4. _____   5. _____   6. _____

CONTENT OF PRAYER REQUEST

_____
_____
_____
_____

THE LORDS ANSWER WAS: DATE: _____ / _____ / _____
YES
NO
NOT YET

HOW THE LORD ANSWERED MY PRAYER

_____
_____
_____
_____

DETAIL OF DELIVERY / LESSON LEARNED

_____
_____
_____
_____

SIGNATURE OF ACCOUNTABILITY _____

Prayer Journal

TITLE: _____ DATE: _____ / _____ / _____

RELEVANT SCRIPTURES:

1. _____ 2. _____ 3. _____
4. _____ 5. _____ 6. _____

CONTENT OF PRAYER REQUEST

_____
_____
_____
_____

THE LORDS ANSWER WAS: DATE: _____ / _____ / _____
YES
NO
NOT YET

HOW THE LORD ANSWERED MY PRAYER

_____
_____
_____
_____

DETAIL OF DELIVERY / LESSON LEARNED

_____
_____
_____
_____

SIGNATURE OF ACCOUNTABILITY _____

PHILIPIANS 4:11 I AM NOT SAYING THIS BECAUSE I AM IN NEED, FOR I HAVE LEARNED TO BE CONTENT WHATEVER THE CIRCUMSTANCES.

Prayer Journal

TITLE: _____ DATE: _____ / _____ / _____

RELEVANT SCRIPTURES:

1. _____ 2. _____ 3. _____
4. _____ 5. _____ 6. _____

CONTENT OF PRAYER REQUEST

_____
_____
_____
_____

THE LORDS ANSWER WAS: DATE: _____ / _____ / _____
YES
NO
NOT YET

HOW THE LORD ANSWERED MY PRAYER

_____
_____
_____
_____

DETAIL OF DELIVERY / LESSON LEARNED

_____
_____
_____
_____

SIGNATURE OF ACCOUNTABILITY _____

Prayer Journal

TITLE: _____ DATE: _____ / _____ / _____

RELEVANT SCRIPTURES:

1. _____ 2. _____ 3. _____
4. _____ 5. _____ 6. _____

CONTENT OF PRAYER REQUEST

_____
_____
_____
_____

THE LORDS ANSWER WAS: DATE: _____ / _____ / _____
YES
NO
NOT YET

HOW THE LORD ANSWERED MY PRAYER

_____
_____
_____
_____

DETAIL OF DELIVERY / LESSON LEARNED

_____
_____
_____
_____

SIGNATURE OF ACCOUNTABILITY _____

PHILIPIANS 4:12 I KNOW WHAT IT IS TO BE IN NEED, AND I KNOW WHAT IT IS TO HAVE PLENTY. I HAVE LEARNED THE SECRET OF BEING CONTENT IN ANY AND EVERY SITUATION, WHETHER WELL FED OR HUNGRY, WHETHER LIVING IN PLENTY OR IN WANT.

Prayer Journal

TITLE: _____   DATE: _____ / _____ / _____

RELEVANT SCRIPTURES:

1. _____ 2. _____ 3. _____
4. _____ 5. _____ 6. _____

CONTENT OF PRAYER REQUEST

_____
_____
_____
_____

THE LORDS ANSWER WAS: DATE: _____ / _____ / _____
YES
NO
NOT YET

HOW THE LORD ANSWERED MY PRAYER

_____
_____
_____
_____

DETAIL OF DELIVERY / LESSON LEARNED

_____
_____
_____
_____

SIGNATURE OF ACCOUNTABILITY _____

Prayer Journal

TITLE: _____ DATE: _____ / _____ / _____

RELEVANT SCRIPTURES:
1. _____ 2. _____ 3. _____
4. _____ 5. _____ 6. _____

CONTENT OF PRAYER REQUEST

_____
_____
_____
_____

THE LORDS ANSWER WAS: DATE: _____ / _____ / _____
YES
NO
NOT YET

HOW THE LORD ANSWERED MY PRAYER

_____
_____
_____
_____

DETAIL OF DELIVERY / LESSON LEARNED

_____
_____
_____
_____

SIGNATURE OF ACCOUNTABILITY _____

PHILIPIANS 4:13 I CAN DO ALL THIS THROUGH HIM WHO GIVES ME STRENGTH.

Prayer Journal

TITLE: _____   DATE: _____ / _____ / _____

RELEVANT SCRIPTURES:

1. _____ 2. _____ 3. _____
4. _____ 5. _____ 6. _____

CONTENT OF PRAYER REQUEST

_____
_____
_____
_____

THE LORDS ANSWER WAS: DATE: _____ / _____ / _____
YES
NO
NOT YET

HOW THE LORD ANSWERED MY PRAYER

_____
_____
_____
_____

DETAIL OF DELIVERY / LESSON LEARNED

_____
_____
_____
_____

SIGNATURE OF ACCOUNTABILITY _____

Prayer Journal

TITLE: _____   DATE: _____ / _____ / _____

RELEVANT SCRIPTURES:

1. _____   2. _____   3. _____
4. _____   5. _____   6. _____

CONTENT OF PRAYER REQUEST

_____
_____
_____
_____

THE LORDS ANSWER WAS: DATE: _____ / _____ / _____
YES
NO
NOT YET

HOW THE LORD ANSWERED MY PRAYER

_____
_____
_____
_____

DETAIL OF DELIVERY / LESSON LEARNED

_____
_____
_____
_____

SIGNATURE OF ACCOUNTABILITY _____

PHILIPIANS 4:14 YET IT WAS GOOD OF YOU TO SHARE IN MY TROUBLES.

Prayer Journal

TITLE: _____ DATE: _____ / _____ / _____

RELEVANT SCRIPTURES:

1. _____ 2. _____ 3. _____
4. _____ 5. _____ 6. _____

CONTENT OF PRAYER REQUEST

_____
_____
_____
_____

THE LORDS ANSWER WAS: DATE: _____ / _____ / _____
YES
NO
NOT YET

HOW THE LORD ANSWERED MY PRAYER

_____
_____
_____
_____

DETAIL OF DELIVERY / LESSON LEARNED

_____
_____
_____
_____

SIGNATURE OF ACCOUNTABILITY _____

Prayer Journal

TITLE: _____   DATE: _____ / _____ / _____

RELEVANT SCRIPTURES:

1. _____ 2. _____ 3. _____
4. _____ 5. _____ 6. _____

CONTENT OF PRAYER REQUEST

_____
_____
_____
_____

THE LORDS ANSWER WAS: DATE: _____ / _____ / _____
YES
NO
NOT YET

HOW THE LORD ANSWERED MY PRAYER

_____
_____
_____
_____

DETAIL OF DELIVERY / LESSON LEARNED

_____
_____
_____
_____

SIGNATURE OF ACCOUNTABILITY _____

PHILIPIANS 4:15 MOREOVER, AS YOU PHILIPPIANS KNOW, IN THE EARLY DAYS OF YOUR ACQUAINTANCE WITH THE GOSPEL, WHEN I SET OUT FROM MACEDONIA, NOT ONE CHURCH SHARED WITH ME IN THE MATTER OF GIVING AND RECEIVING, EXCEPT YOU ONLY;

Prayer Journal

TITLE: _____   DATE: _____ / _____ / _____

RELEVANT SCRIPTURES:

1. _____ 2. _____ 3. _____
4. _____ 5. _____ 6. _____

CONTENT OF PRAYER REQUEST

_____
_____
_____
_____

THE LORDS ANSWER WAS: DATE: _____ / _____ / _____
YES
NO
NOT YET

HOW THE LORD ANSWERED MY PRAYER

_____
_____
_____
_____

DETAIL OF DELIVERY / LESSON LEARNED

_____
_____
_____
_____

SIGNATURE OF ACCOUNTABILITY _____

Prayer Journal

TITLE: _____ DATE: _____ / _____ / _____

RELEVANT SCRIPTURES:

1. _____ 2. _____ 3. _____
4. _____ 5. _____ 6. _____

CONTENT OF PRAYER REQUEST

_____
_____
_____
_____

THE LORDS ANSWER WAS: DATE: _____ / _____ / _____
YES
NO
NOT YET

HOW THE LORD ANSWERED MY PRAYER

_____
_____
_____
_____

DETAIL OF DELIVERY / LESSON LEARNED

_____
_____
_____
_____

SIGNATURE OF ACCOUNTABILITY _____

PHILIPIANS 4: 16 FOR EVEN WHEN I WAS IN THESSALONICA, YOU SENT ME AID MORE THAN ONCE WHEN I WAS IN NEED.

Prayer Journal

TITLE: _____   DATE: _____ / _____ / _____

RELEVANT SCRIPTURES:

1. _____ 2. _____ 3. _____
4. _____ 5. _____ 6. _____

CONTENT OF PRAYER REQUEST

_____
_____
_____
_____

THE LORDS ANSWER WAS: DATE: _____ / _____ / _____
YES
NO
NOT YET

HOW THE LORD ANSWERED MY PRAYER

_____
_____
_____
_____

DETAIL OF DELIVERY / LESSON LEARNED

_____
_____
_____
_____

SIGNATURE OF ACCOUNTABILITY _____

Prayer Journal

TITLE: _____   DATE: _____ / _____ / _____

RELEVANT SCRIPTURES:

1. _____ 2. _____ 3. _____
4. _____ 5. _____ 6. _____

CONTENT OF PRAYER REQUEST

_____
_____
_____
_____

THE LORDS ANSWER WAS: DATE: _____ / _____ / _____
YES
NO
NOT YET

HOW THE LORD ANSWERED MY PRAYER

_____
_____
_____
_____

DETAIL OF DELIVERY / LESSON LEARNED

_____
_____
_____
_____

SIGNATURE OF ACCOUNTABILITY _____

PHILIPIANS 4:17 NOT THAT I DESIRE YOUR GIFTS; WHAT I DESIRE IS THAT
MORE BE CREDITED TO YOUR ACCOUNT.

Prayer Journal

TITLE: _____ DATE: _____ / _____ / _____

RELEVANT SCRIPTURES:

1. _____ 2. _____ 3. _____
4. _____ 5. _____ 6. _____

CONTENT OF PRAYER REQUEST

_____
_____
_____
_____

THE LORDS ANSWER WAS: DATE: _____ / _____ / _____
YES
NO
NOT YET

HOW THE LORD ANSWERED MY PRAYER

_____
_____
_____
_____

DETAIL OF DELIVERY / LESSON LEARNED

_____
_____
_____
_____

SIGNATURE OF ACCOUNTABILITY _____

Prayer Journal

TITLE: _____ DATE: _____ / _____ / _____

RELEVANT SCRIPTURES:

1. _____ 2. _____ 3. _____
4. _____ 5. _____ 6. _____

CONTENT OF PRAYER REQUEST

_____
_____
_____
_____

THE LORDS ANSWER WAS: DATE: _____ / _____ / _____
YES
NO
NOT YET

HOW THE LORD ANSWERED MY PRAYER

_____
_____
_____
_____

DETAIL OF DELIVERY / LESSON LEARNED

_____
_____
_____
_____

SIGNATURE OF ACCOUNTABILITY _____

PHILIPIANS 4:18 I HAVE RECEIVED FULL PAYMENT AND HAVE MORE THAN ENOUGH. I AM AMPLY SUPPLIED, NOW THAT I HAVE RECEIVED FROM EPAPHRODITUS THE GIFTS YOU SENT. THEY ARE A FRAGRANT OFFERING, AN ACCEPTABLE SACRIFICE, PLEASING TO GOD.

Prayer Journal

TITLE: _____   DATE: _____ / _____ / _____

RELEVANT SCRIPTURES:

1. _____   2. _____   3. _____
4. _____   5. _____   6. _____

CONTENT OF PRAYER REQUEST

_____
_____
_____
_____

THE LORDS ANSWER WAS: DATE: _____ / _____ / _____
YES
NO
NOT YET

HOW THE LORD ANSWERED MY PRAYER

_____
_____
_____
_____

DETAIL OF DELIVERY / LESSON LEARNED

_____
_____
_____
_____

SIGNATURE OF ACCOUNTABILITY _____

Prayer Journal

TITLE: _____ DATE: _____ / _____ / _____

RELEVANT SCRIPTURES:
1. _____ 2. _____ 3. _____
4. _____ 5. _____ 6. _____

CONTENT OF PRAYER REQUEST

_____
_____
_____
_____

THE LORDS ANSWER WAS: DATE: _____ / _____ / _____
YES
NO
NOT YET

HOW THE LORD ANSWERED MY PRAYER

_____
_____
_____
_____

DETAIL OF DELIVERY / LESSON LEARNED

_____
_____
_____
_____

SIGNATURE OF ACCOUNTABILITY _____

PHILIPIANS 4:19 AND MY GOD WILL MEET ALL YOUR NEEDS
ACCORDING TO THE RICHES OF HIS GLORY IN CHRIST JESUS.

Prayer Journal

TITLE: _____   DATE: _____ / _____ / _____

RELEVANT SCRIPTURES:

1. _____ 2. _____ 3. _____
4. _____ 5. _____ 6. _____

CONTENT OF PRAYER REQUEST

_____
_____
_____
_____

THE LORDS ANSWER WAS: DATE: _____ / _____ / _____
YES
NO
NOT YET

HOW THE LORD ANSWERED MY PRAYER

_____
_____
_____
_____

DETAIL OF DELIVERY / LESSON LEARNED

_____
_____
_____
_____

SIGNATURE OF ACCOUNTABILITY _____

Prayer Journal

TITLE: _____   DATE: _____ / _____ / _____

RELEVANT SCRIPTURES:

1. _____ 2. _____ 3. _____
4. _____ 5. _____ 6. _____

CONTENT OF PRAYER REQUEST

_____
_____
_____
_____

THE LORDS ANSWER WAS: DATE: _____ / _____ / _____
YES
NO
NOT YET

HOW THE LORD ANSWERED MY PRAYER

_____
_____
_____
_____

DETAIL OF DELIVERY / LESSON LEARNED

_____
_____
_____
_____

SIGNATURE OF ACCOUNTABILITY _____

PHILIPIANS 4:20 TO OUR GOD AND FATHER BE GLORY FOR EVER AND EVER. AMEN.

Prayer Journal

TITLE: _____   DATE: _____ / _____ / _____

RELEVANT SCRIPTURES:

1. _____ 2. _____ 3. _____
4. _____ 5. _____ 6. _____

CONTENT OF PRAYER REQUEST

_____
_____
_____
_____

THE LORDS ANSWER WAS: DATE: _____ / _____ / _____
YES
NO
NOT YET

HOW THE LORD ANSWERED MY PRAYER

_____
_____
_____
_____

DETAIL OF DELIVERY / LESSON LEARNED

_____
_____
_____
_____

SIGNATURE OF ACCOUNTABILITY _____

Prayer Journal

TITLE: _____ DATE: _____ / _____ / _____

RELEVANT SCRIPTURES:

1. _____ 2. _____ 3. _____
4. _____ 5. _____ 6. _____

CONTENT OF PRAYER REQUEST

_____
_____
_____
_____

THE LORDS ANSWER WAS: DATE: _____ / _____ / _____
YES
NO
NOT YET

HOW THE LORD ANSWERED MY PRAYER

_____
_____
_____
_____

DETAIL OF DELIVERY / LESSON LEARNED

_____
_____
_____
_____

SIGNATURE OF ACCOUNTABILITY _____

PHILIPIANS 4:21 GREET ALL GOD'S PEOPLE IN CHRIST JESUS. THE BROTHERS AND SISTERS WHO ARE WITH ME SEND GREETINGS.

Prayer Journal

TITLE: _____   DATE: _____ / _____ / _____

RELEVANT SCRIPTURES:

1. _____ 2. _____ 3. _____
4. _____ 5. _____ 6. _____

CONTENT OF PRAYER REQUEST

_____
_____
_____
_____

THE LORDS ANSWER WAS: DATE: _____ / _____ / _____
YES
NO
NOT YET

HOW THE LORD ANSWERED MY PRAYER

_____
_____
_____
_____

DETAIL OF DELIVERY / LESSON LEARNED

_____
_____
_____
_____

SIGNATURE OF ACCOUNTABILITY _____

Prayer Journal

TITLE: _____   DATE: _____ / _____ / _____

RELEVANT SCRIPTURES:

1. _____ 2. _____ 3. _____
4. _____ 5. _____ 6. _____

CONTENT OF PRAYER REQUEST

_____
_____
_____
_____

THE LORDS ANSWER WAS: DATE: _____ / _____ / _____
YES
NO
NOT YET

HOW THE LORD ANSWERED MY PRAYER

_____
_____
_____
_____

DETAIL OF DELIVERY / LESSON LEARNED

_____
_____
_____
_____

SIGNATURE OF ACCOUNTABILITY _____

Prayer Journal

TITLE: _____ DATE: _____ / _____ / _____

RELEVANT SCRIPTURES:

1. _____ 2. _____ 3. _____
4. _____ 5. _____ 6. _____

CONTENT OF PRAYER REQUEST

_____
_____
_____
_____

THE LORDS ANSWER WAS: DATE: _____ / _____ / _____
YES
NO
NOT YET

HOW THE LORD ANSWERED MY PRAYER

_____
_____
_____
_____

DETAIL OF DELIVERY / LESSON LEARNED

_____
_____
_____
_____

SIGNATURE OF ACCOUNTABILITY _____

Prayer Journal

TITLE: _____ DATE: _____ / _____ / _____

RELEVANT SCRIPTURES:

1. _____ 2. _____ 3. _____
4. _____ 5. _____ 6. _____

CONTENT OF PRAYER REQUEST

_____
_____
_____
_____

THE LORDS ANSWER WAS: DATE: _____ / _____ / _____
YES
NO
NOT YET

HOW THE LORD ANSWERED MY PRAYER

_____
_____
_____
_____

DETAIL OF DELIVERY / LESSON LEARNED

_____
_____
_____
_____

SIGNATURE OF ACCOUNTABILITY _____

Prayer Journal

TITLE: _____ DATE: _____ / _____ / _____

RELEVANT SCRIPTURES:

1. _____ 2. _____ 3. _____
4. _____ 5. _____ 6. _____

CONTENT OF PRAYER REQUEST

_____
_____
_____
_____

THE LORDS ANSWER WAS: DATE: _____ / _____ / _____
YES
NO
NOT YET

HOW THE LORD ANSWERED MY PRAYER

_____
_____
_____
_____

DETAIL OF DELIVERY / LESSON LEARNED

_____
_____
_____
_____

SIGNATURE OF ACCOUNTABILITY _____

Prayer Journal

TITLE: _____ DATE: _____ / _____ / _____

RELEVANT SCRIPTURES:

1. _____ 2. _____ 3. _____
4. _____ 5. _____ 6. _____

CONTENT OF PRAYER REQUEST

_____
_____
_____
_____

THE LORDS ANSWER WAS: DATE: _____ / _____ / _____
YES
NO
NOT YET

HOW THE LORD ANSWERED MY PRAYER

_____
_____
_____
_____

DETAIL OF DELIVERY / LESSON LEARNED

_____
_____
_____

SIGNATURE OF ACCOUNTABILITY _____

Prayer Journal

TITLE: _____   DATE: _____ / _____ / _____

RELEVANT SCRIPTURES:

1. _____ 2. _____ 3. _____
4. _____ 5. _____ 6. _____

CONTENT OF PRAYER REQUEST

_____
_____
_____
_____

THE LORDS ANSWER WAS: DATE: _____ / _____ / _____
YES
NO
NOT YET

HOW THE LORD ANSWERED MY PRAYER

_____
_____
_____
_____

DETAIL OF DELIVERY / LESSON LEARNED

_____
_____
_____
_____

SIGNATURE OF ACCOUNTABILITY _____

Prayer Journal

TITLE: _____ DATE: _____ / _____ / _____

RELEVANT SCRIPTURES:

1. _____ 2. _____ 3. _____
4. _____ 5. _____ 6. _____

CONTENT OF PRAYER REQUEST

_____
_____
_____
_____

THE LORDS ANSWER WAS: DATE: _____ / _____ / _____
YES
NO
NOT YET

HOW THE LORD ANSWERED MY PRAYER

_____
_____
_____
_____

DETAIL OF DELIVERY / LESSON LEARNED

_____
_____
_____
_____

SIGNATURE OF ACCOUNTABILITY _____

Prayer Journal

TITLE: _____ DATE: _____ / _____ / _____

RELEVANT SCRIPTURES:

1. _____ 2. _____ 3. _____
4. _____ 5. _____ 6. _____

CONTENT OF PRAYER REQUEST

_____
_____
_____
_____

THE LORDS ANSWER WAS: DATE: _____ / _____ / _____
YES
NO
NOT YET

HOW THE LORD ANSWERED MY PRAYER

_____
_____
_____
_____

DETAIL OF DELIVERY / LESSON LEARNED

_____
_____
_____
_____

SIGNATURE OF ACCOUNTABILITY _____

Prayer Journal

TITLE: _____ DATE: _____ / _____ / _____

RELEVANT SCRIPTURES:

1. _____ 2. _____ 3. _____
4. _____ 5. _____ 6. _____

CONTENT OF PRAYER REQUEST

_____
_____
_____
_____

THE LORDS ANSWER WAS: DATE: _____ / _____ / _____
YES
NO
NOT YET

HOW THE LORD ANSWERED MY PRAYER

_____
_____
_____
_____

DETAIL OF DELIVERY / LESSON LEARNED

_____
_____
_____
_____

SIGNATURE OF ACCOUNTABILITY _____

Prayer Journal

TITLE: _____   DATE: _____ / _____ / _____

RELEVANT SCRIPTURES:

1. _____ 2. _____ 3. _____
4. _____ 5. _____ 6. _____

CONTENT OF PRAYER REQUEST

_____
_____
_____
_____

THE LORDS ANSWER WAS: DATE: _____ / _____ / _____
YES
NO
NOT YET

HOW THE LORD ANSWERED MY PRAYER

_____
_____
_____
_____

DETAIL OF DELIVERY / LESSON LEARNED

_____
_____
_____
_____

SIGNATURE OF ACCOUNTABILITY _____

Prayer Journal

TITLE: _____   DATE: _____ / _____ / _____

RELEVANT SCRIPTURES:

1. _____ 2. _____ 3. _____
4. _____ 5. _____ 6. _____

CONTENT OF PRAYER REQUEST

_____
_____
_____
_____

THE LORDS ANSWER WAS: DATE: _____ / _____ / _____
YES
NO
NOT YET

HOW THE LORD ANSWERED MY PRAYER

_____
_____
_____
_____

DETAIL OF DELIVERY / LESSON LEARNED

_____
_____
_____
_____

SIGNATURE OF ACCOUNTABILITY _____

Prayer Journal

TITLE: _____   DATE: _____ / _____ / _____

RELEVANT SCRIPTURES:

1._____ 2._____ 3._____
4._____ 5._____ 6._____

CONTENT OF PRAYER REQUEST

_____
_____
_____
_____

THE LORDS ANSWER WAS: DATE: _____ / _____ / _____
YES
NO
NOT YET

HOW THE LORD ANSWERED MY PRAYER

_____
_____
_____
_____

DETAIL OF DELIVERY / LESSON LEARNED

_____
_____
_____
_____

SIGNATURE OF ACCOUNTABILITY _____

Prayer Journal

TITLE: _____ DATE: _____ / _____ / _____

RELEVANT SCRIPTURES:

1. _____ 2. _____ 3. _____
4. _____ 5. _____ 6. _____

CONTENT OF PRAYER REQUEST

_____
_____
_____
_____

THE LORDS ANSWER WAS: DATE: _____ / _____ / _____
YES
NO
NOT YET

HOW THE LORD ANSWERED MY PRAYER

_____
_____
_____
_____

DETAIL OF DELIVERY / LESSON LEARNED

_____
_____
_____
_____

SIGNATURE OF ACCOUNTABILITY _____

Prayer Journal

TITLE: _____ DATE: _____ / _____ / _____

RELEVANT SCRIPTURES:

1. _____ 2. _____ 3. _____
4. _____ 5. _____ 6. _____

CONTENT OF PRAYER REQUEST

_____
_____
_____
_____

THE LORDS ANSWER WAS: DATE: _____ / _____ / _____
YES
NO
NOT YET

HOW THE LORD ANSWERED MY PRAYER

_____
_____
_____
_____

DETAIL OF DELIVERY / LESSON LEARNED

_____
_____
_____
_____

SIGNATURE OF ACCOUNTABILITY _____

Prayer Journal

TITLE: _____ DATE: _____ / _____ / _____

RELEVANT SCRIPTURES:

1. _____ 2. _____ 3. _____
4. _____ 5. _____ 6. _____

CONTENT OF PRAYER REQUEST

_____
_____
_____
_____

THE LORDS ANSWER WAS: DATE: _____ / _____ / _____
YES
NO
NOT YET

HOW THE LORD ANSWERED MY PRAYER

_____
_____
_____
_____

DETAIL OF DELIVERY / LESSON LEARNED

_____
_____
_____
_____

SIGNATURE OF ACCOUNTABILITY _____

Prayer Journal

TITLE: _____ DATE: _____ / _____ / _____

RELEVANT SCRIPTURES:

1. _____ 2. _____ 3. _____
4. _____ 5. _____ 6. _____

CONTENT OF PRAYER REQUEST

_____
_____
_____
_____

THE LORDS ANSWER WAS: DATE: _____ / _____ / _____
YES
NO
NOT YET

HOW THE LORD ANSWERED MY PRAYER

_____
_____
_____
_____

DETAIL OF DELIVERY / LESSON LEARNED

_____
_____
_____
_____

SIGNATURE OF ACCOUNTABILITY _____

Prayer Journal

TITLE: _____ DATE: _____ / _____ / _____

RELEVANT SCRIPTURES:

1. _____ 2. _____ 3. _____
4. _____ 5. _____ 6. _____

CONTENT OF PRAYER REQUEST

_____
_____
_____
_____

THE LORDS ANSWER WAS: DATE: _____ / _____ / _____
YES
NO
NOT YET

HOW THE LORD ANSWERED MY PRAYER

_____
_____
_____
_____

DETAIL OF DELIVERY / LESSON LEARNED

_____
_____
_____
_____

SIGNATURE OF ACCOUNTABILITY _____

Prayer Journal

TITLE: _____   DATE: _____ / _____ / _____

RELEVANT SCRIPTURES:

1. _____ 2. _____ 3. _____
4. _____ 5. _____ 6. _____

CONTENT OF PRAYER REQUEST

_____
_____
_____
_____

THE LORDS ANSWER WAS: DATE: _____ / _____ / _____
YES
NO
NOT YET

HOW THE LORD ANSWERED MY PRAYER

_____
_____
_____
_____

DETAIL OF DELIVERY / LESSON LEARNED

_____
_____
_____
_____

SIGNATURE OF ACCOUNTABILITY _____

Prayer Journal

TITLE: _____ DATE: _____ / _____ / _____

RELEVANT SCRIPTURES:

1. _____ 2. _____ 3. _____
4. _____ 5. _____ 6. _____

CONTENT OF PRAYER REQUEST

_____
_____
_____
_____

THE LORDS ANSWER WAS: DATE: _____ / _____ / _____
YES
NO
NOT YET

HOW THE LORD ANSWERED MY PRAYER

_____
_____
_____
_____

DETAIL OF DELIVERY / LESSON LEARNED

_____
_____
_____
_____

SIGNATURE OF ACCOUNTABILITY _____

Take Us To Church

Prayer Journal

TITLE: _____ DATE: ___/___/___

SPEAKER: _____

SERMON: _____ BOOK OF: _____

SERMON NOTES:
_____
_____
_____
_____
_____
_____
_____

PERSONAL REFLECTIONS:
_____
_____
_____
_____
_____
_____
_____
_____

Prayer Journal

TITLE: _____ **DATE:** ___/___/___

SPEAKER: _____

SERMON: _____ **BOOK OF:** _____

SERMON NOTES:

_____
_____
_____
_____
_____
_____
_____
_____

PERSONAL REFLECTIONS:

_____
_____
_____
_____
_____
_____
_____
_____

Prayer Journal

TITLE: _____ DATE: ___/___/___

SPEAKER: _____

SERMON: _____ BOOK OF: _____

SERMON NOTES:
_____
_____
_____
_____
_____
_____
_____

PERSONAL REFLECTIONS:
_____
_____
_____
_____
_____
_____
_____
_____
_____

Prayer Journal

TITLE: _____ DATE: ___/___/___

SPEAKER: _____

SERMON: _____ BOOK OF: _____

SERMON NOTES:

_____
_____
_____
_____
_____
_____
_____
_____

PERSONAL REFLECTIONS:

_____
_____
_____
_____
_____
_____
_____
_____
_____

Prayer Journal

TITLE: _____ DATE: ___/___/____

SPEAKER: _____

SERMON: _____ BOOK OF: _____

SERMON NOTES:
_____
_____
_____
_____
_____
_____
_____

PERSONAL REFLECTIONS:
_____
_____
_____
_____
_____
_____
_____
_____

Prayer Journal

TITLE: _____ DATE: ___/___/___

SPEAKER: _____

SERMON: _____ BOOK OF: _____

SERMON NOTES:
_____
_____
_____
_____
_____
_____
_____
_____

PERSONAL REFLECTIONS:
_____
_____
_____
_____
_____
_____
_____
_____

Prayer Journal

TITLE: _____ DATE: ___/___/___

SPEAKER: _____

SERMON:_____ BOOK OF:_____

SERMON NOTES:

_____
_____
_____
_____
_____
_____
_____
_____

PERSONAL REFLECTIONS:

_____
_____
_____
_____
_____
_____
_____
_____
_____
_____

Prayer Journal

TITLE: _____ DATE: ___/___/___

SPEAKER: _____

SERMON: _____ BOOK OF: _____

SERMON NOTES:
_____
_____
_____
_____
_____
_____
_____
_____

PERSONAL REFLECTIONS:
_____
_____
_____
_____
_____
_____
_____
_____
_____

Prayer Journal

TITLE: _____ **DATE:** ___/___/___

SPEAKER: _____

SERMON: _____ **BOOK OF:** _____

SERMON NOTES:
_____
_____
_____
_____
_____
_____
_____
_____

PERSONAL REFLECTIONS:
_____
_____
_____
_____
_____
_____
_____
_____
_____

Prayer Journal

TITLE: _____ DATE: ___/___/___

SPEAKER: _____

SERMON: _____ BOOK OF: _____

SERMON NOTES:
_____
_____
_____
_____
_____
_____
_____
_____

PERSONAL REFLECTIONS:
_____
_____
_____
_____
_____
_____
_____
_____
_____
_____

Prayer Journal

TITLE: _____ DATE: ___/___/____

SPEAKER: _____

SERMON: _____ BOOK OF: _____

SERMON NOTES:
_____
_____
_____
_____
_____
_____
_____

PERSONAL REFLECTIONS:
_____
_____
_____
_____
_____
_____
_____
_____
_____

Prayer Journal

TITLE: _____ DATE: ___/___/___

SPEAKER: _____

SERMON: _____ BOOK OF: _____

SERMON NOTES:
_____
_____
_____
_____
_____
_____
_____

PERSONAL REFLECTIONS:
_____
_____
_____
_____
_____
_____
_____
_____

Prayer Journal

TITLE: _____ DATE: ___/___/___

SPEAKER: _____

SERMON: _____ BOOK OF: _____

SERMON NOTES:
_____
_____
_____
_____
_____
_____
_____
_____

PERSONAL REFLECTIONS:
_____
_____
_____
_____
_____
_____
_____
_____
_____
_____

Prayer Journal

TITLE: _____ DATE: ___/___/____

SPEAKER: _____

SERMON: _____ BOOK OF: _____

SERMON NOTES:
_____
_____
_____
_____
_____
_____
_____
_____

PERSONAL REFLECTIONS:
_____
_____
_____
_____
_____
_____
_____
_____

Prayer Journal

TITLE: _____ DATE: ___/___/___

SPEAKER: _____

SERMON: _____ BOOK OF: _____

SERMON NOTES:
_____
_____
_____
_____
_____
_____
_____

PERSONAL REFLECTIONS:
_____
_____
_____
_____
_____
_____
_____
_____
_____

Prayer Journal

TITLE: _____ DATE: ___/___/____

SPEAKER: _____

SERMON: _____ BOOK OF: _____

SERMON NOTES:
_____
_____
_____
_____
_____
_____
_____
_____

PERSONAL REFLECTIONS:
_____
_____
_____
_____
_____
_____
_____
_____
_____
_____

Prayer Journal

TITLE: _____ DATE: ___/___/___

SPEAKER: _____

SERMON: _____ BOOK OF: _____

SERMON NOTES:
_____
_____
_____
_____
_____
_____
_____

PERSONAL REFLECTIONS:
_____
_____
_____
_____
_____
_____
_____
_____
_____

Prayer Journal

TITLE: _____ DATE: ___/___/____

SPEAKER: _____

SERMON: _____ BOOK OF: _____

SERMON NOTES:

_____
_____
_____
_____
_____
_____
_____

PERSONAL REFLECTIONS:

_____
_____
_____
_____
_____
_____
_____
_____
_____

Prayer Journal

TITLE: _____ DATE: ___/___/___

SPEAKER: _____

SERMON: _____ BOOK OF: _____

SERMON NOTES:
_____
_____
_____
_____
_____
_____
_____
_____

PERSONAL REFLECTIONS:
_____
_____
_____
_____
_____
_____
_____
_____
_____

Prayer Journal

TITLE: _____ DATE: ___/___/___

SPEAKER: _____

SERMON: _____ BOOK OF: _____

SERMON NOTES:
_____
_____
_____
_____
_____
_____
_____
_____

PERSONAL REFLECTIONS:
_____
_____
_____
_____
_____
_____
_____
_____
_____

Prayer Journal

TITLE: _____ DATE: ___/___/___

SPEAKER: _____

SERMON: _____ BOOK OF: _____

SERMON NOTES:
_____
_____
_____
_____
_____
_____
_____

PERSONAL REFLECTIONS:
_____
_____
_____
_____
_____
_____
_____
_____
_____

Prayer Journal

TITLE: _____ DATE: ___/___/___

SPEAKER: _____

SERMON: _____ BOOK OF: _____

SERMON NOTES:
_____
_____
_____
_____
_____
_____
_____
_____

PERSONAL REFLECTIONS:
_____
_____
_____
_____
_____
_____
_____
_____

Prayer Journal

TITLE: _____ DATE: ___/___/____

SPEAKER: _____

SERMON: _____ BOOK OF: _____

SERMON NOTES:
_____
_____
_____
_____
_____
_____
_____

PERSONAL REFLECTIONS:
_____
_____
_____
_____
_____
_____
_____
_____
_____

Prayer Journal

TITLE: _____ DATE: ___/___/___

SPEAKER: _____

SERMON: _____ BOOK OF: _____

SERMON NOTES:
_____
_____
_____
_____
_____
_____
_____

PERSONAL REFLECTIONS:
_____
_____
_____
_____
_____
_____
_____
_____

Prayer Journal

TITLE: _____ DATE: ___/___/___

SPEAKER: _____

SERMON: _____ BOOK OF: _____

SERMON NOTES:
_____
_____
_____
_____
_____
_____
_____

PERSONAL REFLECTIONS:
_____
_____
_____
_____
_____
_____
_____
_____

Prayer Journal

TITLE: _____ DATE: ___/___/___

SPEAKER: _____

SERMON: _____ BOOK OF: _____

SERMON NOTES:

_____
_____
_____
_____
_____
_____
_____
_____
_____

PERSONAL REFLECTIONS:

_____
_____
_____
_____
_____
_____
_____
_____
_____

Prayer Journal

TITLE: _____ DATE: ___/___/___

SPEAKER: _____

SERMON: _____ BOOK OF: _____

SERMON NOTES:
_____
_____
_____
_____
_____
_____
_____

PERSONAL REFLECTIONS:
_____
_____
_____
_____
_____
_____
_____
_____
_____
_____

Prayer Journal

TITLE: _____ DATE: ___/___/____

SPEAKER: _____

SERMON: _____ BOOK OF: _____

SERMON NOTES:

_____
_____
_____
_____
_____
_____
_____
_____

PERSONAL REFLECTIONS:

_____
_____
_____
_____
_____
_____
_____
_____
_____
_____
_____

Prayer Journal

TITLE: _____ DATE: ___/___/____

SPEAKER: _____

SERMON: _____ BOOK OF: _____

SERMON NOTES:
_____
_____
_____
_____
_____
_____
_____

PERSONAL REFLECTIONS:
_____
_____
_____
_____
_____
_____
_____
_____
_____

Prayer Journal

TITLE: _____ DATE: ___/___/___

SPEAKER: _____

SERMON: _____ BOOK OF: _____

SERMON NOTES:

_____
_____
_____
_____
_____
_____
_____

PERSONAL REFLECTIONS:

_____
_____
_____
_____
_____
_____
_____
_____

Prayer Journal

TITLE: _____ DATE: ___/___/___

SPEAKER: _____

SERMON: _____ BOOK OF: _____

SERMON NOTES:
_____
_____
_____
_____
_____
_____
_____

PERSONAL REFLECTIONS:
_____
_____
_____
_____
_____
_____
_____
_____
_____

Prayer Journal

TITLE: _____ **DATE:** ___/___/___

SPEAKER: _____

SERMON: _____ **BOOK OF:** _____

SERMON NOTES:
_____
_____
_____
_____
_____
_____
_____
_____

PERSONAL REFLECTIONS:
_____
_____
_____
_____
_____
_____
_____
_____

Prayer Journal

TITLE: _____ DATE: ___/___/___

SPEAKER: _____

SERMON: _____ BOOK OF: _____

SERMON NOTES:
_____
_____
_____
_____
_____
_____
_____

PERSONAL REFLECTIONS:
_____
_____
_____
_____
_____
_____
_____
_____
_____

Prayer Journal

TITLE: _____ DATE: ___/___/____

SPEAKER: _____

SERMON: _____ BOOK OF: _____

SERMON NOTES:
_____
_____
_____
_____
_____
_____
_____
_____

PERSONAL REFLECTIONS:
_____
_____
_____
_____
_____
_____
_____
_____
_____
_____

Prayer Journal

TITLE: _____ DATE: ___/___/____

SPEAKER: _____

SERMON: _____ BOOK OF: _____

SERMON NOTES:
_____
_____
_____
_____
_____
_____
_____

PERSONAL REFLECTIONS:
_____
_____
_____
_____
_____
_____
_____
_____
_____

Prayer Journal

TITLE: _____ DATE: ___/___/___

SPEAKER: _____

SERMON: _____ BOOK OF: _____

SERMON NOTES:
_____
_____
_____
_____
_____
_____
_____
_____

PERSONAL REFLECTIONS:
_____
_____
_____
_____
_____
_____
_____
_____
_____
_____

Prayer Journal

TITLE: _____ DATE: ___/___/___

SPEAKER: _____

SERMON: _____ BOOK OF: _____

SERMON NOTES:

_____
_____
_____
_____
_____
_____
_____
_____

PERSONAL REFLECTIONS:

_____
_____
_____
_____
_____
_____
_____
_____
_____

Prayer Journal

TITLE: _____ DATE: ___/___/____

SPEAKER: _____

SERMON: _____ BOOK OF: _____

SERMON NOTES:
_____
_____
_____
_____
_____
_____
_____
_____

PERSONAL REFLECTIONS:
_____
_____
_____
_____
_____
_____
_____
_____
_____
_____

Prayer Journal

TITLE: _____ DATE: ___/___/___

SPEAKER: _____

SERMON: _____ BOOK OF: _____

SERMON NOTES:
_____
_____
_____
_____
_____
_____
_____

PERSONAL REFLECTIONS:
_____
_____
_____
_____
_____
_____
_____
_____
_____

Prayer Journal

TITLE: _____ DATE: ___/___/____

SPEAKER: _____

SERMON: _____ BOOK OF: _____

SERMON NOTES:
_____
_____
_____
_____
_____
_____
_____

PERSONAL REFLECTIONS:
_____
_____
_____
_____
_____
_____
_____
_____
_____

Prayer Journal

TITLE: _____ DATE: ___/___/____

SPEAKER: _____

SERMON: _____ BOOK OF: _____

SERMON NOTES:
_____
_____
_____
_____
_____
_____
_____

PERSONAL REFLECTIONS:
_____
_____
_____
_____
_____
_____
_____
_____
_____

Prayer Journal

TITLE: _____ DATE: ___/___/___

SPEAKER: _____

SERMON: _____ BOOK OF: _____

SERMON NOTES:
_____
_____
_____
_____
_____
_____
_____

PERSONAL REFLECTIONS:
_____
_____
_____
_____
_____
_____
_____
_____
_____

Prayer Journal

TITLE: _____ DATE: ___/___/___

SPEAKER: _____

SERMON: _____ BOOK OF: _____

SERMON NOTES:
_____
_____
_____
_____
_____
_____
_____
_____

PERSONAL REFLECTIONS:
_____
_____
_____
_____
_____
_____
_____
_____
_____
_____

Prayer Journal

TITLE: _____ DATE: ___/___/____

SPEAKER: _____

SERMON: _____ BOOK OF: _____

SERMON NOTES:
_____
_____
_____
_____
_____
_____
_____
_____

PERSONAL REFLECTIONS:
_____
_____
_____
_____
_____
_____
_____
_____
_____
_____

Prayer Journal

TITLE: _____ DATE: ___/___/___

SPEAKER: _____

SERMON: _____ BOOK OF: _____

SERMON NOTES:
_____
_____
_____
_____
_____
_____
_____

PERSONAL REFLECTIONS:
_____
_____
_____
_____
_____
_____
_____
_____

Prayer Journal

TITLE: _____ DATE: ___/___/___

SPEAKER: _____

SERMON: _____ BOOK OF: _____

SERMON NOTES:
_____
_____
_____
_____
_____
_____
_____

PERSONAL REFLECTIONS:
_____
_____
_____
_____
_____
_____
_____
_____

Prayer Journal

TITLE: _____ DATE: ___/___/____

SPEAKER: _____

SERMON: _____ BOOK OF: _____

SERMON NOTES:
_____
_____
_____
_____
_____
_____
_____

PERSONAL REFLECTIONS:
_____
_____
_____
_____
_____
_____
_____
_____

Prayer Journal

TITLE: _____ DATE: ___/___/___

SPEAKER: _____

SERMON: _____ BOOK OF: _____

SERMON NOTES:
_____
_____
_____
_____
_____
_____
_____

PERSONAL REFLECTIONS:
_____
_____
_____
_____
_____
_____
_____
_____
_____

Prophetic Dreams & Notes

Notes

Notes

Notes

Notes

Notes

Notes

Notes

Notes

Notes

Notes

Notes

Notes

Notes

Notes

Notes

Notes

Notes

Notes

Notes

Notes

GGPJ Men's Biblical Puzzle

Across
4. Something you must do to get into heaven it starts with an F
5. Brothers betrayed him
9. False Evidence appearing real
10. Built a ark
11. Basic instructions before leaving earth
12. On the 3rd Day
15. The Lord is my banner
16. The writer of psalms

Down
1. The first woman
2. Parted the Red Sea
3. The last book in the New Testament of the Bibl
5. God my healer
6. Speaking to God
7. The pieces you put together
8. Holy Spirit
13. Better than sacrifice

CEDRIC B. GLOVER

About the Authors

Cedric Glover, is a father of three, a husband, and now having written his first piece of literature, he has become a published author. His journey to becoming an author was quite unconventional as he was inspired by his wife, Imani M-Glover, who wrote her second book "Glorifying Grace Prayer Journal" which published January 2019. In his spare time, Cedric sells real-estate, he is on the Deacon Board at his church, Acts Full Gospel Church of God in Christ. He works as a platform engineer. He also enjoys spending time with his three sons and beautiful wife of almost 20 years. His plans for the future include more prayer based literature geared towards helping writers in their walk with the Lord Jesus Christ.

Contact Imani & Cedric Glover
Email: imanimglover@yahoo.com
Website: www.imanimglover.com.

IMANI M-GLOVER

About the Author

Imani M-Glover is a California native who resides in the Bay Area with her husband, two sons, and a bonus baby. She is the author of two books, the first being a collaborative work titled, "Before the Vows Break " which shares tales of triumph

and gives advice to wives and wives to be. Her second piece of literature "Glorifying Grace Prayer Journal" is a faith based Journal which helps readers in their walk of faith by recording prayer requests and giving believers a place to document their faithfulness of the Lord.

Imani is also the owner of The Lemonade Bar located in Oakland California. The next time you are in The Bay area look her up and have a refreshing drink!

Contact Imani
Email: imanimglover@yahoo.com
Website: www.imanimglover.com.

www.ingramcontent.com/pod-product-compliance
Lightning Source LLC
Chambersburg PA
CBHW032050150426
43194CB00006B/483